# LAKSHMI UNBOUND

# LAKSHMI UNBOUND

Sanjukta Dasgupta

Chitrangi

**Published by:** *Chitrangi*, A-10/1, Amarabati, Sodepur, Calcutta 700110.

**First edition:** March, 2017

**Printed at:** S. P. Communications

**Contact**
Email: thethirdeyeimprint@gmail.com



**Cover design:** Bitan Chakraborty

**ISBN**-13: 97893-85782-73-2

**Price:** INR 200

Chitrangi Foundation is a colloborative effort by
**Hawakal Publishers & Shambhabi Imprint**

For my five- month old granddaughter
*Ivaana (Ubuntu)*

With the hope that the liberated Lakshmis
in the Twenty First Century can bask in the
pristine environment  of  complete social,
intellectual and creative freedom.

January 5, 2017

# A Few Words...

*Lakshmi Unbound* is a freedom song. It is the song that resonates in the recesses of the mind, it is an anthem that is heard by the spirit that longs to break free from the binding chains of callous habit and social conditioning.

In the Introduction of his four-act lyrical drama *Prometheus Unbound,* the English romantic poet of the nineteenth century Percy Bysshe Shelley had observed that it would have been impossible for him to reconcile the Oppressor with the Champion of humankind. Shelley's reluctance becomes doubly pertinent in *Lakshmi Unbound,* as many of the poems in this volume trace how oppression and cultural claustrophobia destroy the creative talents of the women who can dream, imagine and desire to change the world.

Each year on October 11, The United Nations celebrates The Day of the Girl Child. The Sustainable Development Goals of the United Nations has set a target that by 2030, all girl children should be given equal opportunities for education, health and employment without any gender discrimination. Women's rights and human rights are synonymous and women must be recognized as human beings and not as sexualized human bodies. Till we are able to make this distinction between women's bodies and women's identity, aware women know that the battle must go on.

Some might even ask- but what has poetry got to do with gender sensitization? One may state unequivocally, that it is poetry and other literary genres that can open up doors and windows of the fossilized mind which can lead to women's liberation after centuries of exploitation and barbaric violence.

*Lakshmi Unbound* however does not restrict itself to addressing women's entrapment within the patriarchal power structure. Many of the poems in my fifth volume pace beyond the boundaries of the known spaces, trying to hear the sounds of silence as the trees stand tall, flowers blossom, dew drops fall, birds fly and streams flow without any self-proclamation.

The poems in this volume as in the earlier ones such as *Snapshots, Dilemma, First Language* and *More Light* endeavour to find a way out of the encircling gloom. These poems can be described as poems of resistance, they often conduct a severe introspection that hinges on despair and depression. But the poems also catch a glimpse of the radiance that illuminates though the tantalizing ray of freedom can even be illusory.

The poems in *Lakshmi Unbound* engage in the pursuit of enlightenment that can lead to freedom from bondage imposed on women for biological reasons. The passionate desire to gain freedom proves that once the local Lakshmi and the global Angel in the House are able to unbind themselves, they can become active agents of social change. When Virginia Woolf had stated that the formula for creative freedom was to eliminate the Angel in the House, it was a path-breaking statement from one of twentieth century's peerless feminists. So Woolf announced categorically, "Killing the Angel in the House was part of the occupation of a woman writer". Explaining the importance of this homicidal advice, Woolf explained that such violence as murder could be undertaken in self-defense, "Had I not killed her, she would have killed me. She would have plucked the heart out of my writing".

It is with this necessity to eliminate in order to liberate that I wish to share the thirty-one poems that are included in my fifth volume of poems, *Lakshmi Unbound*.

Sanjukta Dasgupta
February 28, 2017

# CONTENTS

# LAKSHMI UNBOUND:
# A SOLILOQUY

" Killing the Angel in the House was
part of the occupation of a woman
writer"

*Virginia Woolf*


"With downcast eyes and veiled head
I have spent twenty-two years in your house
That's why both at home and without
Everyone says I am *Lakshmi, Sati*
An extremely good woman!"

*Freedom ( Mukti  Rabindranath Tagore)*


Don't, don't, call me Lakshmi
I can't ever be Lakshmi
I want to fly kites
I want to climb trees
I want to read and write
I want to sing and dance
I want to climb mountains
I want to swim in the seas

I want to do what I like
*Whenever I like*


I want to be mad
I want to be bad
I can't be in corners of four walled spaces
I can't be in eddies
I want to flow in the mainstream
I want to be in whirlpools
I want to roam and run
I want to eat fruits from trees
I want to drink to the last drop
The juice of grapes
I want to cook *for myself*
I want to dream
I want to pace the rainbow arch
In a spectacular hallucination


I can't be Lakshmi

I will ever fail this endurance test
I have to speak
I have to cry
I have to scream
I have to laugh
I have to swim in rivers
I cannot swim in pools
I want to fly like an eagle
I want to glide like a feather


I will forever fail this endurance test

I have flung off the Sellotape on my lips
I will sing the freedom song
I may not be Lakshmi
*But I am*
I just can't be Lakshmi
I have to break the silence
My wealth is not jewels
My wealth is my gipsy spirit


I can't be Lakshmi
I can't be good, sane, silent Lakshmi
I can't be the Angel in someone's house
I don't want to be a disembodied spirit
I don't want to be Lakshmi
I am *Alakshmi*
Trap me if you can!

# MRINAL'S FIRST LETTER

*Era jail khanake bole Sasur Bari*
( Tagore *Tasher Desh*)
( *They call jails marital homes*)


No one could believe
That gentle Mrinal who obeyed
All the rules of the sacred space
Would write a letter to her husband

Mrinal did write poems
No one saw them
No one read them
They would have sniggered
If they were told
That good Mrinal wrote poems!

Crazy, crazy, Crazy
A wife composing poems
Pitiable plight of a childless woman
They said as they sighed
Then destitute Bindu
Became Mrinal's companion
Alas soon Bindu was coerced into marriage
Married to a violent insane man

Helpless Bindu set herself on fire
*Setting herself on fire*
*Was considered by some*
*As the height of fashion-*
Tagore's scathing irony
Defined Mrinal's life story

Sad self immolation
Of young innocent Bindu
Who had loved Mrinal so well
But then immolation was not unknown
So many, so many were barbecued alive
On the barbaric pyres of their dead husbands

Mrinal like her elder sister Nora
In a far away world
Shut herself out from the hypnotic
Humiliating, terrifying sacred space
Mrinal erased the lines of control

Mrinal spread her arms like wings
She spun wildly on her toes
Her heart sang like a Koel in spring
As she mailed her first letter
To her husband of fifteen years-

*'But I shall not return to 27, Makhan Baral Lane*
*ever again*
*I saw what happened to Bindu.*
*I have realized the position women have in this*
*society.*
*I don't want to go through it anymore'*

Mrinal celebrated her freedom
 From the insecure shelter
Under her husband's feet
As she scripted her resignation letter.

(Inspired by Rabindranath Tagore's short story
*Streer Patra* ( The Wife's Letter)

# CHANDALIKA

Untouchable!
Away, away
Out of sight
Outcast Chandalika
Caste had cast her out

*Dalit, dalit, dalit*
Trampled, tortured, terrified
Accursed Chandalika shrank
Bewildered and helpless

Chandalika
Born in a Sudra home
Bearing a name like a badge of shame
Ostracized Chandalika
A young girl who never did smile

Then out of the horizon
Stepped steadily towards her
The serene and wise monk
Ananda met Chandalika

So long invisible, untouchable
Accursed Chandalika

Doomed and damned from
The day she was born

For the first time
In her wretched miserable life
Chandalika saw a smile
A smile that was not a sneer

 The monk's gentle smile
Soothed her insulted soul
Healed her humiliated pores
The caring voice asked her
For some water to slake the thirst

Water touched by a Sudra!
Unholy water contaminated
By the dalit girl's innocent touch
The voices of power and privilege
Shouted and screamed
With horror and hatred
But the monk smiled and coaxed her
For water to slake his thirst

At last Chandalika raised
Her bowed head high
The smile of the merciful monk
Was like the radiance
Of a thousand suns
Chandalika
Dalit maiden branded and stigmatized
Innocent yet condemned
Condemned for being born in a home

Not by her choice!

 Now Chandalika
Stood tall bathed
 In the pristine shower
Of radiant rays
Traumatised Chandalika
After many, many centuries
Smiled  at last
For the sun also did rise for her.

(inspired by Rabindranath Tagore's dance
drama *Chandalika*)

# CHITRANGADA

Princess of Manipur
Swift arrows fly from her bow
Her lithe body like a flying javelin
Zooms through the foliage

Warrior prince Arjun is her target
The arrows become flowers
In her scented hair
Drugged by love and desire
Warrior princess Chitrangada
Becomes lovelorn Radha

But Arjun is insatiable
The desirable luscious fruit
Is just dessert, hunger  now rises
For a glimpse of the warrior princess

That wish too is fulfilled
Chitrangada the seductress
Now becomes Arjun's partner
For better or for worse

The warrior princess's caveat
To the warrior prince melted the lines of control
*Let us be equal partners in peace and war*

*Let us entwine arms, stand side by side*

Self assurance, dignity and tender grace
Bonded the lovers
*"I have many flaws and blemishes*
*I am a traveller in the great world-path,*
*My garments are dirty*
*And my feet are bleeding with thorns"*
 Softly murmured
The Bard of Santiniketan's  Chitra


Powerful yet not conceited
The visionary poet's Chitra
The Princess of Manipur
Also the princess of the people
Scripted a mantra for every woman,
Princess or pauper-
*"I am Chitra. No goddess to be worshipped, nor yet*
*The object of common pity to be brushed aside*
*Like a moth, with indifference. "*


Reference:

Tagore Rabindranath  "Chitra" a play in *The
English Writings of Rabindranath Tagore* volume
2 New Delhi: Sahitya Akademi, 2001. The
Bengali play is titled, "Chitrangada".

# GORA'S RE-BIRTH

*"Ma, you are my real mother"*
The orphan youth exclaimed
As he felt free at last
A surrogate son
Liberated forever
From the maze and myopia
Of pride and prejudice
Icons and idols.

Unfettered Gora, at last stood tall
He felt weightless like a feather riding
A wind-chariot on an azure autumn sky
*"He had no mother, no father, no country, no caste,*
*No name, no family , no gotra, no deity"*

All those self inflicted taboos
Became irrelevant
As Gora was re-born
When he said he would drink water
Brought in by the untouchable Lachhmia-
*"Ma, please send for your Lachhmia now.*
*Ask her to fetch me some water"*

Anandamoyee smiled
It was strange that the simple truth
She had known so well

And had practiced lifelong
To realize the same truth
Gora took such a laborious route
At last Gora sensed
Lachhmia and the rarefied Lakshmi
Are indissoulbly bound

Unchained from limiting scriptures
 Gora was born again
In a pristine world
Of unfettered knowledge
Where the mind is fearless
This time he chanted without inhibition
The magic mantra of limitless freedom

Excerpts are from Rabindranath
Tagore's novel *Gora* translated by Radha
Chakravarty.

# A TALE OF A SLEEPING VILLAGE

*A sleeping village grew guns…*


Suddenly a sleeping village
Was invaded with multi-coloured flags
The farms grew guns that year

Farmers dreamt of an eternal satellite city
Pavements of gold and clang of steel
A spectacular wake-up call

A sleeping village
Alas slept too well
To scan the doublespeak

A sleeping village slept on alas
Duped by wheels of verbal spin
Lured by the lullaby of mercurial promises

Simple villagers grew guns that year
Learnt to press fingers on triggers
While the ploughs gathered dust

A sleeping village
Saw death that year
"Leave us alone", they wailed

Seduced by those who lie like truth
Promised dreams were really nightmares
They writhed in the satanic grip

A sleeping village
Drenched in blood and tears
Grew three crops- guns, bullets and bombs

Smart strangers with honeyed tongues
Drugged by the dizzy web of words
From residents to refugees overnight

Fear stalked them all as the
Power sports went on
A flying bullet, a house on fire
Bomb blasts and the hush of death

Narcotized messenger boys and girls,
Mother Courage in a trance
In a tropical village
Brecht and Gorky's mothers
Trapped by puppeteers

This sleeping village
Suddenly disappeared one midnight

Like a flying saucer, with all its people,
All its land and dug up trenches
This sleeping village
Fell asleep again
And heaved a sigh of relief

*Awakening had been bitter and terrifying*

# REFUGEES
## and Deja Vu

So long it had been the *firangis* who did it
But once they went
We do it to our own, for their good

Women, men and children
Ran out of their own homes and land
Seeking refuge in camps

All of them were of the wrong colour
So were their ducks, hens, goats, cows
But they stole their livestock despite the hated colour

Not the timeless war between brand names of Gods
But the seduction for more, instantly some more
Made them puppets of cold-blooded politics

Dazed by the word-jugglers
Long-distance compassion
Misguided efforts

They shot each other on their beloved land
Pathetic puppets with primitive symbols
Sickle, hammer, rods and spears

But in real  use
Were rocket launchers, landmines
AK47s and other swanky toys of death

The good earth became a killing field
Neighbours became enemies overnight
Ishwar and Allah were summoned to divide further
Those who had lived in peace so long

Even the refugee camps were invaded
Peace became a tearful prayer for
Refugees in their home places

Those who manipulated the gullible marionettes
Had dreams of conquest
Their capital this time was of course ignorance


*Those we thrust into our backyards*
*They are the ones who pull us back-*
The wisdom of the poet's words of long ago

So fearfully distorted
Revised and twisted into a time-serving
Grotesque pastiche, a charade
A nightmare pretending to be a wake-up call!

# SECOND COMING

The ghastly silhouette of strange ships
Suddenly darkening the horizon
Lethal specks, and lies like truth
Narcotized natives surrendered

Strange tongues called them Calibans
Land, home and selves
Owned unfairly by fair aliens
That of course was in times past

Times present is about the world in every home
Power a seductive illusion
The strange ships are phantoms now
Playful spiders in the world wide web

Windows are not magic casements
Not just forlorn fairy lands in cyber space
Real, virtual, touchable,
Untouchable fairy tales
Fact, fiction, texts, textiles, fabric, fabrication

Fused or de-centred by the strange violence
Of dreams that are nightmares for others
Provocative dream peddlers
Promise profit and power
While Ozymandias of Egypt groans again!

# A NEW DAWN

"Yes, I am an untouchable, and every Negro
in the United States of America is an
untouchable."
Martin Luther King:
From sermon at Ebenezer Baptist Church,
July 4, 1965


That hate could be about pigmentation
I learnt first as a schoolgirl
Reading *Uncle Tom's Cabin*

Hate transformed into empathy
*The Adventures of Huckleberry Finn*
Redeemed hope

That hate could be so relentless
I learnt from *Roots*,
A tale of miserable uprooting
Mercifully, soon I learnt about warriors too

Rosa Parks, Langston Hughes,
Paul Robeson, Malcolm X
And the curious visitor to India–
Martin Luther King
Introduced as a *Dalit* in a school classroom

Five decades later the chemistry of black and
white
Has created this one pathfinder
Who chants the mantra of *Change*

He stood tall that triumphant night
A Lighthouse in the encircling gloom
Connecting all, not some.

No new Martin Luther King
Will ever have to declare-
"Yes, I am an untouchable, and every Negro
 In the United States of America is an
untouchable"


A spectacular new Rainbow House
A confluence of colours and cultures
Melting binaries forever

Audaciously dreaming of a world
Where all colours will blend and dance
In the radiant swirl

Peace, happiness and prosperity
Will return to the pristine earth
And poets will write again

Not about bombs, guns and blasts
Not about limbs, fractures and body bags
Not about shattered minds
And horrible trauma

Poets will hail the new dawn of hope
Tinkle of a rare mellifluous music
Of the linked human chain

A trailblazing journey
Of discovery, recovery
And a healing beyond
Human words

"The principal introduced me and then as he came to the conclusion of his introduction, he says, "Young people, I would like to present to you a fellow untouchable from the United States of America." And for a moment I was a bit shocked and peeved that I would be referred to as an untouchable..."

From *The Autobiography of Martin Luther King, Jr*, Chapter 13 –'Pilgrimage to Non-Violence'.
 Martin Luther King Jr visited India in 1959 accompanied by  his wife Correta King and a few others.

# FESTIVE SEASON

Sweet season of feasts
Season of fun and treats
Seasoned and sautéed so long
Strangely the stranglehold of stress
Evaporates with the approaching
Sound of drumbeats

Members of the divine first family
Arrive in state in the state
Appalled at the distressed statecraft
Desperate in quest of the healing
State of the art that can reinstate
The pristine power and glory
In every dreaming heart

Season of bliss and joy
Ten arms suddenly become
Millions of protecting arms
Holding each one in a soft clasp
A touch so tender and tranquil
Like the flowing of the ancient river
On a lazy winter starlit evening
And a misty moon

Less than one hundred hours of annual
autumnal fiesta
Enchants, engulfs, empowers, departs

Renewing its pledge to return again and again
Renewal and the new melt and fuse
As the spear strikes the erring heart and mind
Diabolic shouts of laughter
Become penitent whimpers
The discerning radiant rays
Of a thousand suns
Scorch and illuminate in one fell sweep
Of a lightning strike.

# FESTIVAL OF LIGHTS

Suddenly a moonless night each year
Becomes a radiant day
Each dark corner twinkles
Sparkling homes, dazzling clothes
Tinkling laughter
A magic wand transforms all

At midnight the grand Goddess Kali
Is invoked to bless the good earth
Kali's blood smeared scimitar
Glistens in the air
The sound of drumbeats,
The carefree laughter of children
Animates the midnight prayers

 Homely Lakshmi ushers wealth
On this night of the festival of lights
Kali and Lakshmi share the same day-filled night
Lights dazzle and crackers boom
Scintillating glow deafening sound
Is Lakshmi light and Kali sound
Energy of Kali and the benign grace of Lakshmi
A strange mix and match
As the rhythmic drumbeats
Reverberate through the joyous air

A thin young mother
With her toddler daughter and wee son
Suddenly raises her arms and dances bare-feet
Her toddlers sway in step,
Thrilled and fascinated
As their loving mother swirls
With the enchanting drumbeats,
A beatific smile lights up
The dancing woman's careworn face

As the sound of crackers boom,
Tired oil lamps flicker
As the electric lights in homes
Twinkle through the night
The young woman in a dirty faded sari
And an oversized blouse
Dances and dances and dances
Under the flyover,
Which has been her home for a while.

# GIRL CHILD

*"Daddy, when I grow up will I become a girl"*

The innocent cherubic child
Swayed and rocked in a cradle
Lullaby soothing the little ears
 Very soon the child ran
Faster than the wind
Climbed up the trunk
Of the tall tree

But then someone whispered
"No, no this one is not a child
This little tender thing is a girlchild."
Girlchild, girlchild
The echoes were like the hiss of snakes
Prison chains clanged eagerly
Every song became a 'no" song
For the little girlchild

She will have no childhood
As she was born a girl
What or who is a Girl
How does one become a girl
Why can't she be a child

"Why am I in a cage with a signboard

'GIRLCHILD' "
 She asked as she learnt to fight
Without weapons or shield

Braveheart girlchild
Nurtured by many, many girls
 A sorority comprising all ages
Mother, sisters, aunts
Female teachers, friends,  colleagues
Stood up again and again
Tall, scarred , ravaged
Smiling, sure and undefeated.

*" Daddy, when I grow up will I become a girl"*
*( This question used as an epigraph was addressed to*
*a Professor of English by his very young school going*
*daughter)*

## I KILLED HIM M'LORD

For seventeen years
My body was a punching bag
My ears were sore with sores
The  violent volley of filthy words
My eyes were like a hunted deer
I could not hide nor run away
My home was my
Rigorous imprisonment cell

Yet at daytime he was so calm, so caring
Running his fingers on the red stripes of my
back
The fingers went forward
like a tram on burnt red tracks
His fingers played like a child
Running a toy car on the parent's back.
He promised like everytime
That it wouldn't happen again
But in the evening someone else
Seemed to return home
As if he was possessed,
He dashed towards me
Hit me with his favourite book
The *Selected poems of John Donne*

This was the poet that brought us together

As we read, sang and danced during our
college days
But for seventeen years the poet remained
unread
Gathering dust within a bookshelf of
forgotten books
But tonight he had a different look
He picked up the large knife in the kitchen
And ran towards my only son, our son,
Our thirteen year old boy he had named JOY

As he lunged towards our boy,
My only child, my only son
My only joy and solace
Some power thrust
The grinding stone into my hand
I hit him on his head with all my strength
Amit fell on the floor and yet tried to rise

I wrenched the knife from his hand
And stabbed him in his stomach
I stabbed him, stabbed, stabbed, stabbed
Till Amit's mother pulled me off

My son stood like a statue
I did not cry My Lord
I could not cry
But I could dial 100
The police came
And now I stand before you
As a university graduate
I know the punishment for murder

As a Judge you know the punishment
For domestic violence
Do whatever your profession dictates
*I killed him my Lord*

( News in *Times of India Ei Samay* April 16,
2016, Shreya Chakraborty killed Shantanu
Chakraborty. Supported by mother in law
Gouri. Marriage of 25 years)

# RAPE

He was so much stronger
He did what he has done
For centuries and centuries
Lust, power and passionless thrust

She was so much weaker
He did what he had come to do
He had to prove he was a peacock
He had to prove she was a sacrificial lamb

He gnashed his teeth
Eyes gleaming like a hunter on a kill
He felt omnipotent
As she writhed and screamed
Hate in every curve of her ravished frame

When he left
He warned and snarled
He said he would come back
He was not quite done yet
Not grateful, just gratified

She dragged her bruised body
To the phone on the table
The police officer said,

" You must have provoked him
He is a good man"

She stood upright now
Waiting for him
Waiting for them
Spitting on the floor
Laughing at her bare body

She knew now
She would win this game
She waited
She dreamt-

*Like a screw top bottle cap*
*His head lay on the floor*
*Eyes wide open*
*In stark disbelief*
She smiled when
He came in as in the past
Afterwards he went away
Defiant and proud, as always

But this time
A strange serene smile lit her face
At last she could dare to desire
His severed head at her feet.

# SINDOOR

The tribal chief
Etched a path of blood
The middle parting
Of a head full of flowing hair
Proudly beamed the sign
Of being claimed by a man
A coded sign
Signed in blood
Commanding fidelity
Branded bonded labour
Dutiful wife, mother
Compulsory roles dictated
By the red line in the hair parting.

Then with the march of time
Vermillion powder
Symbol of the redness of fresh blood
Slick  sindoor lining
The middle parting of a head of hair
 Symbol of pride and power for some
For some a sign of slavery

For some a cosmic sign
For some a cosmetic change

The red path
In the middle parting
Of the dark tresses
Seemed helpless
As the blood flowed
From the wounds
As the red blood dripped within
Invisible internal haemorrhage
As the battered body
Sank with relief
Into the arms of Mother Earth
The union of myth and now.

# THE ELEVENTH MUSE

Be it Calliope, Clio, Erato
Euterpe, Melpomene, Polyhymnia
Or even Terpsichore, Thalia or Urania
The elegant Nine Muses were dedicated
To muscular arms and strong fingers
The creative power pen
Had to be mightier than the sword
Those virile creators
Narrated epics, sagas
 Lyrics, elegies, hymns, songs and dance
Tragedy, Comedy,  Astronomy
Scripted sonorous journeys of  discovery
 Timeless trails of  self-discovery
Those inspired ones
 Who wrote chauvinist epics and sagas
Composed heroic poetry and the alexandrine

Poets waited with patience or impatience
For the playful, elusive Muse
Passionate poets invoked
With anxiety and longing
The graceful mesmeric Muse
Dreams born on the page as words
Enabled by the Muse's  magic invisible touch

Words, words, words
Grew like a golden harvest
Swaying in the spring or autumn breeze
At ease, at ease
As the Muse touched the tip of the quill pen
Or guided the masculine fingers gently
Ever so gently
Enabling the birth of a new poem.

Remember, Shakespeare suddenly claimed a
Tenth Muse
His thirty eighth sonnet cheerfully invoked
The new Muse, ten times more powerful

*Be thou the tenth muse, ten times more in worth*
*Than those old nine which rhymers invocate;*

But The Bard of Avon's Tenth Muse
 Was not Sappho, Plato's Tenth Muse,
The mortal muse or was she?

The graceful feminine Muses were so elusive
So exclusive in their devotion
 They pampered  poets who were invariably
their Other
 No time for those poets who were their own
kin
Poets who were often invisible till after death
Poets who wrote in secret, wrote in fear
Poets who changed their own names
In order to create or compose
 Poets who were terrified that they were

Poets – guilty yet irrepressible
Some had tongues lopped off
 Others were insulted tortured ridiculed
For they dared to create
These poor, penniless poets

Such are the poets who write in secrecy
For they are poets who cook
Millions of meals
Poets who bear and raise children
Poets  who die in childbirth
Poets who nurture adults
In a place called home
Poets who do not claim independence
Poets who passionately desire
Interdependence

Such have been those
Poets who reached out
To an androgynous spirit
As their enabling mesmeric Muse
These poets yearned for an icon
The poets needed a profile
They longed ardently for an image, a symbol
For an inclusive androgynous Muse
Hermaphrodite – but could there be a Muse
Closer to the soil, closer to home
They pondered as they waited

Then in a dream suddenly flashed
The astonishing  figure
Of divine togetherness

"Ardhanariswar! Ardhanariswar!"
The poets exclaimed with joy
We have searched for you
Among the icons of the West
While you were here, shy, gentle, elusive
Yet proud and powerful
Waiting for us to claim you
OUR very own Eleventh Muse
Admirable *Ardhanariswar*
Entwined in an union of energy and grace
Invincible  Eleventh Muse
Bonding and binding
Poets of the past, present and future
Without bias or prejudice
In a level  creative garden of jouissance.

All the poets now invoked
The Eleventh Muse
The shy, sure and steady Muse
Of an ancient land
*Ardhanariswar,*
The androgynous creative spirit
The inspirational Eleventh Muse.

# LOVE POEM

After all each poem
Is a poem of love

Without love
Every morning, every day, every evening

Would just trickle like water through a sieve
No one and nothing to love except oneself

Love rises like a thousand suns
Love's silken moonbeams brighten dark night

Each dark corner shines like a diamond
Love's teasing smile
Between forever and never

Love is a warm clasp of an invisible hand
Of an unseen friend

Love is a storm that rushes through homes
and hearts
Opening barred windows and doors,
Melting rusty locks with a magic touch

Is L/O/V/E- lonely, only, violent, emotion
Is L/O/V/E- longing, oneness, vibrant, energy

Love is the sport we play lifelong
Where the winner takes nothing

Love is a game that has no rules
Love all, advantage lovers
Seduced by deuce and tie-breakers

Game point, set point
All unsettled by a single shy look

The world falls apart or is re-born
As the fingers entwine in silent dialogue

Love is a dew-drenched rosebud at midnight
Lovelorn night strains nightlong
To eye the radiant dawn

Timeless lovers are like day and night
Forever together and forever apart

So don't tease me to write a love poem
What else can I write?

# LET'S GO

Like a drop of dew
On the palm of my hand
Your face

Like a floating feather
Your words on ether
Your touch

Like a raging storm
Through a deserted house
Your absence

Let us then go, you and I
Out of the last days of this year
Into a timeless oasis

Let the magic carpet
Fly us out of calendar time
And all those days, dates, weeks and months

Let us go where spoken words
Are flowers and not tangled webs
Of deceit, conceit and poisonous pride

Let us go then you and I
To that haven where peace
Sparkles like a sunlit pool

Let us go, let's go, let's go
All of us and you and I
As the reindeer tinkles its silver bells

Its time, its time, its time
To fly beyond the ticking of watches
To watch the arrival of the infant Saviour

Let's ride the colour-splashed rainbow
Let's dive into the oceans of hope
Let's forget tomorrow, now is the only time!

STAIRCASE

Stepping carefully
Down the broad stately staircase
Will no longer be watched
By a pair of beautiful young eyes
Waiting with a smile
At the landing

 This afternoon
It was such a lonely
Stepping down the stairs
Suddenly the smiling face flitted
For a mercurial moment
And then it was
Just a bare staircase

Hand in hand
With loneliness
Stepping more carefully
For there's no one to warn
That rash rush is not
For mellow years
No one to carry the bag of books
The tools of the trade

And though the steps
Will learn that there's no one waiting
The heart rises with joy
As it sees in the horizon
A new rainbow
Arching a new beginning

Moist misty eyes
Through the glistening raindrops
The dusk lengthens into dawn
A turning point
A journey begins
The young lieutenant
Like a shaft of light
Brightens the hazy horizon
While shadows lengthen here

Alas, letting go is not easy at all!

# ODE TO SILENCE

Sounds of silence
Trickled like silent tear drops
On a monsoon midnight
Sounds of silence
Echoed as the blossoms of winter
Drooped and dropped
Tear-drops on a frosty night
Enchained words on silent pages
Not the tapping sound
Of fingers on a keyboard
Nor the scraping noise
Of pen on paper
Silent sighs
Tense and intense
In search of mercurial silence
Elusive erratic silence
Darting like a golden deer
A fleeting flash of silence
Among the swarming sounds
Encircled by cacaphony
A floating island of silence .

As silent as a voiceless tree on a traffic island
A Stoic sentinel smiling at human hurry
A committed commotion

Of sound in motion
Silence like a secret wafting fragrance
Silence like a wisp of cotton
 Silence like a fairy boat in mid-air
Silence is the voice within
As our entwined fingers chat voicelessly
As a tender hug or a gentle pat
Composes symphonies of silent touch
Between the drums of thunderous sound
Fragile silence curls precariously
Like a sleepy child in need of rest.

# ODE TO SOUND

Not the eerie uncanny sound of silence
Sounds that swirl but never bite
Not the serpentine silence
In slithering motion
Dancing to the monotonous tune
Of the snake charmer's flute sounds
Not silence like a dormant volcano
Nor a venomous viper in repose
Secure sound of a teaspoon
Stirring the sugar in a cup
Sound of a tram car clanging its bells
Or is it a signature song
Of the Streetcar Named Desire?
Sounds of tinkling and clanging bells
In a merry go round
Rhapsody, symphony and a concert of voices
Discordance in the heart of concord
The silence of lost words
Reclaimed by a babel of voices
What's in a sound?
Perhaps it's a vocal dream
Perhaps it is just some din
A vociferous statement
Bridging life and oblivion.

# HOPE

Like a dead crow in the debris
Stink of rotting flesh and feathers

All desires hurtle towards
Putrid stench and nauseating despair

Violent retching
A rash spreads all over

Yet from such excrescence
Arises a faint but firm hope

The end of someone
The end of something

It not the end of everything
The dreadful dead-end
A triumphant turning point

# POET'S SONG

He asked:
Why don't you sing songs of NOW?
All your songs are songs of THEN

The poet said:
All my life
I tried to build bridges between THEN and
NOW

Is there THEN and NOW
In the infinite blue sky above
Calendars in the blue expanse
Of oceans and seas

Is it a new sky
Is it an old ocean

All my life
I tried to tie the strains of songs

Bridging the old and new
Like a glorious rainbow

Arching promises of a new world
The unknown desiring to become known

The known as mysterious as the unknown
Strangeness in the familiar

The unfamiliar sending out signals
Till old and new, known and unknown

The familiar and the unfamiliar
Blend and bond, share and care

Daring to venture into the not yet definable
Caring to create links
Between the self and others:

The poet then picked up
A fallen dry bright yellow leaf
From the path on which she stood

A wild, playful wind snatched it from her
hand
The bright yellow leaf became a sky-boat

The poet saluted the old leaf
On its new journey

# POEM WITHIN

A poem within
Needs to be let out

Wrapped in words
Signifying something

The poet struts and frets
Staging nothing

The poem seems passive but steady
A pillar of support or protest

A poem not a garland of words
A life jacket for the marooned soul

A poem a crutch, a baton
A poem a flower not a whip

The poem within
The poem on the page

A poem quits the poet's womb
Severs the umbilical cord

Out in the storm and tsunami waves
The poet's poem survives, revives

Decay and death snuff out the poet
More often without a memorial stone

Yet like a speck of sparkling diamond
The inviolate poem will linger somewhere

As long as words survive...

# A POEM A DAY
# KEEPS THE PSYCHIATRIST AWAY

Each day
I write a poem
The wise ones
Interpret this
Overflow as
Active passivity
Passive activity
An aspirant's
Inept word-play

But I am helpless
I can just write a few lines
I can't use an AK 47
I don't know how to use it
I can't even buy it
Its too costly for my slender purse
And I can't stand blood splattered bodies
I can't stand torn limbs, open skulls
I can't stand faces
Arrested in grotesque grimace
Of sudden death

The pen is mightier than the sword
Pen pushers declare in self conceit

But the sword gnashes
Its ferreted nuclear teeth
Tanks, bombs, bazookas, drones
Torpedoes, submarines, F 16, RDX
Lethal toys for killer adults
More grisly than the violent video games
In hot pursuit of oil wells or just to sustain
Activity in the market of military hardware

Dipping my pen in the stench pool
Of victims' fluids
I write everyday
I have to write everyday
I just have to keep on writing
Blindfolded in a tunnel
With no light
My words are hopeless scribbles
I ask everyone
Is the madhouse
This one here
Around me, ahead of me
Behind me
Or is it that the walled
Central Institute of Psychiatry
The lunatic asylum
In *Kanke* in neighbouring Jharkhand
Looking for me!

# BOVINE EXPORTS

*One man's meat is another man's poison*
*One man's food is another man's faith*
*One man's dream is another man's dread*

Last evening on TV news
We saw some poor women being thrashed
For ferrying meat named BEEF
For sale in the market
Later laboratory tests
Announced that the meat
The women ferried was not flesh of cows
The meat the women ferried was
The flesh of buffaloes
As both cows and buffaloes
Are members of the bovine family
The generic name for their mutual flesh
Is Beef.


Google The Omniscient Deity of
Information
Had another surprise just waiting to be
searched.
INDIA till last year has been
The LARGEST exporter of BEEF In the
world.
Milk of cows is expensive and elite

Milk of buffaloes is for us, Dalits
If only the bovine animals could speak
If only they could have responded
To the debates in Parliament
About holy cows and dispensable buffaloes


What semantic jugglery
And language strategies
A plate of roasted beef can be
Either cow meat or buffalo meat
No one will flinch an inch
In the name of religion if it is the latter
No one will flinch or lynch anyone
For eating fish
Thank God fish are of
Infinite sizes and shapes
Too swift and slippery to be sacred
So eating fish is still a gastronomic delight
And not a cause for assault
And homicidal urges

Plotting politicians have made
Our plate of meat
A dreadful slice of hate and death
The taste buds shrivel in shock and dismay
At the violent vagaries of the inhuman race.

# TALAQ

The most dreadful word in family life throughout the world is Divorce. Notice the phonetic impact of the Anglo Saxon signifier-DIVORCE..The Bengali synonym BICHEDDH is also phonetically a rasping word, as is the Arabic word *Talaq*

What a verbal explosive
In a disyllabic word
Uttered like a
Cruel chant of power
Three times.
Breaking the brittle
Seal of wedlock.
Three times
He shouted
*Talaq*
*Talaq*
*Talaq*

Thrice she cried out
No
No
No

But NO was not a shield
That could save her
From the blast
Of talaq
This lethal verbal trident
Devastated dependent wives
Traumatised helpless children

Her grandmother was talaq-ed
Her mother was talaq-ed
So many grandmothers
So many wives
So many sisters
Bore the whip lash
Of a single word-*Talaq*

Mohsina
Did not know
She made history in 2016
As from her parents home
She called her dowry-greedy husband
She switched on the speaker
Of her mobile phone

The entire assembled village panchayat
Comprising villagers of all religions
Both women and men
Heard for the first time
After centuries of silence
And scalding silent tears
A young woman
Spit out with confidence

*Talaq, talaq, talaq*

The leaves of the sentinel trees
Rustled in approval
The flying birds sang with delight
The moist monsoon breeze
Blew so gently, so gently
Like a mother's caress
Soothing a suffering child


The speaker phone
Spat out the same word thrice
Mohsina uttered that terrible word
Without hesitation
Without trepidation
Without vaccilation
Everyone heard and agreed
Everyone nodded
In unflinching assent

What a joyous turn
Of the wheel of history
Mohsina had called her husband
On the mobile phone
To create history
The simple village girl
Simply said
Loud and clear
Just three times
*"Talaq*

*Talaq*
*Talaq*"

'Then she disconnected the line'[1]

[1]Written after reading the report titled, "Bride Turns Dowry tables on Groom" by Piyush Srivastava ( July 25, Lucknow) In The Telegraph Kolkata, July 26, 2016.

# FEAR

"present fears are less than horrible
imaginings"

Macbeth Act 1, Scene 3

Fear is the silent stalker
That follows me everywhere
All the time, anytime
It leers and lurks
In the merciless maze
Of the eyeless mind

Fear seals my lips
Fear gags my mouth
Fear throttles me
Fear chokes my words
Fear forces my eyes shut
Fear makes me pretend
I haven't heard anything
I haven't seen anything
I haven't felt anything

Fear has made me senseless
Like a rotten log on a patch
Of rain drenched grass
Fear has slashed off my tongue
Fear just makes me moan and groan

Inarticulate muffled whimpers
Spine-chilling uncanny whispers

Fear shrivels and shrinks me everyday
Fear has bent my backbone
Fear has bent my head
Fear makes my nerves tingle
Fear makes my blood go cold
Dwarfed and devastated by fear
I join the ghastly procession
Of terrified robots

Like a menacing monarch
Fear smiles and sneers
As it twiddles and turns
The remote control
In its scaly claws
I tremble and cringe in fear
And yet....

I am trying to stand up!

# LAUGHTER

I haven't laughed for a long long time
I haven't heard my voice rise and fall
In delight, in reckless joy
Caught in a paroxysm of convulsive laughter

Laughter rising out of me
Like a flowing fountain of wordless sounds
Laughter so infectious
That the world bursts out laughing

Pandemic laughter
Surging, surfing
Like an assembly of chirping birds
That rise with the dawn

Laughter
Laughed at me
As I laughed off
The lies and tears
Laughter
Could not stop itself
As the earth shook
The clouds burst
The rains rushed down
In laughing silver sheets

Laughter
Cascading in carefree impulse
Laughed as if
There would be no tomorrow
Laughter trickled
Laughter rippled
Laughter cooled
All storms in tea cups
Laughter lovingly and laughingly
Had the last laugh!

# PERSPECTIVE


On hearing a poet read with pride his
Bangla poem eulogising the secure
Space of the toilet for philosophical
Reflections and meditation

*Such alas is the politics and play of*
*unreliable perspectives.*


Because it varies
Despite spectacles
Perspectives differ
Perspectives challenge
Perspectives provoke debate
Instill resistance
Deconstruct stereotypes
Perspectives protect power
Perspectives enforce power
Perspectives can also be blind
Perspectives project selfish self-interest.

Such is the variable
In the inconstant perspectives
A toilet to a MCP poet
Is a haven of relief
And Greek philosophy

So the space for effluents
The space within closed doors
The poet calls a toilet
Has a ceramic chair with a hole


Alas, the toilet
Is not just about
A ceramic chair with a hole
For a woman or a woman poet
This one space
Where the door can be locked
Without seeking permission
From self-proclaimed authority
Is the space of catharsis
A space of pity and tears
A space to shudder unnoticed
A space to silently express repulsion and fear
A space to smile at oneself in the bathroom mirror
A space to touch the reflected face brimming with tears
A space to touch and taste the salty trickle
A space where tears seem like bleeding drops of blood

Alas, even a toilet generates gendered perspectives
A man's intimate, private space of philosophy
Is a woman's private space for silent expression
Of trauma, fears and oceans of tears.

# TRANSLATION

*Lost in translation?*

When we met
Our mutual words transcended
Transformed in translation
We strung words like pearls
Mother tongue and Other tongue
A new poem born out of the womb
Of a well known old poem
The original homegrown poem
Became a global sapling
Rooted, uprooted, re-rooted
Unique avatar

Linguistic transfer
Cultural code switching
Those are puzzles for sages
And heat oppressed brains
Ethnic poems in global syntax
Global poems in ethnic inscription
Smiled in the new dawn
Reaching hearts and minds
Liberated from the intense entrapment
 In either/or- singular tongues

Our willing translations
Our mutual spinning of words
In an Other tongue, in our mother tongue
To fill the gaps others hadn't bridged
Insularity and isolation were erased
A rainbow of words
Not a chaotic Babel
Brought us together

Isolated islands of words
Converged into continents of communion
We never regretted any loss in translation
We were incorrigible dreamers, for us
Territories and borders were life- threatening
We dreamt about bringing together
A fractured world with our healing words—
*Vasudhaiva Kutumbakum*
Our world as a single family

In translation
We gained an inclusive world
We mingled diversity and difference
In our several tongues and daring dreams
We translated uninhibited
For us, to be transfixed and immobile
Was surrender and suicide
We translated and translated and translated
And our mutual words
Became universal symbols,
Signs and signposts
Our adhesive translations made
The Other our own
Fused into a holistic dream come true

Translated, we became indivisible
Not you and me, but us.